FE in the 21st Century

What's in it for adults?

Report from
NIACE Conference Triad

Ian Nash and Sue Jones

niace

promoting adult learning

Published by

promoting adult learning

© 2008 National Institute of Adult Continuing Education
(England and Wales)
21 De Montfort Street   2 006 001 785
Leicester
LE1 7GE

Company registration no. 2603322
Charity registration no. 1002775

NIACE has a broad remit to promote lifelong learning opportunities
for adults. NIACE works to develop increased participation in
education and training, particularly for those who do not have easy
access because of class, gender, age, race, language and culture, learning
difficulties or disabilities, or insufficient financial resources.

You can find NIACE online at www.niace.org.uk

ISBN 978 1 86201 365 0

Design, typeset and printed by Prestige Colour Solutions Ltd, Leicester

CONTENTS

FOREWORD

From November 2007 to January 2008, NIACE held three conferences on the theme *FE in the 21st Century: what works for adults?* The first was "Learning from the Past: what to adopt and what to avoid", chaired by Paul Mackney, Associate Director (FE) NIACE. The second was "The Present: what to cherish and what to ditch", chaired by Leisha Fullick, Pro-director (London) – Institute of Education. The third was "Preparing for the Future: what to fight for and what to resist", chaired by Alan Tuckett, Director of NIACE.

Conference participants analysed the circumstances around the loss of one million learners in two years following the development of Government policy in favour of skills for the workplace, led by employer demand. During the course of the conferences, John Denham, Secretary of State for the new Government Department for Innovation, Universities and Skills, announced a review of adult learning provision.

The conferences reflected both the participants' enthusiasm for adult education in FE Colleges and mounting concern about its marginalisation under the agenda set by the Foster and Leitch reports.

There were remarkably rich contributions at the conferences which have been compiled in this NIACE report by Ian Nash and Sue Jones (www.nashandjones.co.uk).

These conferences were designed to feed into NIACE's detailed Inquiry into the Future of Lifelong Learning.

We have included as an appendix John Denham's invitation to contribute to the Government's consultation on informal learning in full, though the consultation document itself can be found at www.adultlearningconsultation.org.uk.

One practical result of the ideas generated at these conferences has been the development by NIACE of the FE Adult Learning Network for Practitioners to protect, develop and enhance adult education as a comprehensive lifelong learning entitlement. Anyone interested in joining the network should contact: paul.mackney@niace.org.uk.

Paul Mackney.

CHAPTER I

HOW WE CAME TO BE WHERE WE ARE

A future based on experience, not grounded in amnesia

Further education for adults is at the crossroads, having lost one million learners from colleges in two years following the Government's shift of focus from broad education to skills for employability. With the Foster inquiry into the future of colleges trumpeting economically useful skills for youth and the Leitch report stressing economically useful skills for adults, many people have fallen through the gap between the two, as public funds for everything else have been reduced and adult education fees are being increased.

While significant growth in government funding for colleges has come over the past eight years, money was diverted to skills from what politicians euphemistically described as "other" learning, suggesting that nothing of serious merit or need would be lost. But NIACE challenged that view in two reports: *Eight in Ten* (2005) and *The Road to Nowhere* (2007) which identified the key role "other" learning played in getting marginalised adults onto the skills ladder. *Eight in Ten*, the report of an independent inquiry, stressed the need for "new thinking and new vocabulary" around adult learning. The need for what became known as personal, community and development learning was greater not less than the Government envisaged, as the two NIACE reports amply demonstrated.

Chairing the first of three conferences, *FE in the 21st Century*, Paul Mackney (Associate Director FE, NIACE) declared that the big questions now were: "How does all this affect the groups that colleges have served in the past? What is going to be the effect of having a new Government department for adults (the Department for Innovation, Universities and Skills)? In which direction should adult learning be moving?" There were hints at the time of the conference that the new Secretary of State, John Denham, would turn a critical eye to the Leitch recommendations and look again at the value of "other" adult learning experiences. While this did not indicate a U-turn from the skills agenda, Denham's promise of a major inquiry into adult learning did suggest that the new administration was keen to take stock.

There was unanimous agreement at all three conferences that past experiences offered crucial lessons for the Government. Paul Mackney said: "NIACE believes it is most important that those experiences are taken into account. We need a future based on experience, not grounded in amnesia. This needs careful consideration of all the evidence. The stonemasons of the Isle of Purbeck have a saying: 'When you are young you look at a stone once and hit it 20 times; when older you look at it 20 times and hit it once.' We still appear to be in the multiple-hitting phase."

Did anything really change?

So, will politicians stand back with the mallet and chisel? There was a clearly perceived desire, voiced at the conferences, for them to intervene less and trust the professionals more. This arose from the perception that, since the late 1980s, adult learners had become pawns on the policy chessboard, moved around at the whim of politicians to suit one strategy then another. For college governors, directors, managers and staff alike, their job is now to marshal, train and sustain those pieces to meet whatever targets were set them. This had led to a sense of frustration, palpable among speakers and other conference participants, that their professional judgment was increasingly sidelined.

When the Conservative Government removed colleges from local authority control and made them independent corporations, under in the 1992 Further and Higher Education Act, business was given a controlling interest on governing boards. Intense competition among colleges followed, with no central planning or catchment areas. "Market forces would drive out weak and unresponsive colleges and reward stronger ones," Alan Birks stated. Pressure was on colleges for greater "efficiency" – everyone was expected to do more for less. "With incorporation, there was a testosterone-fuelled rush to be the most hard-line college – a real temptation to "have a go" by 'liberated' principals who saw other colleges and staff as the opposition," said Caroline Gray, curriculum manager at City College Birmingham. Industrial strife, strikes and redundancies followed, as the national pay structure and local authority Silver Book contracts were torn up, and lecturers were reappointed on lower pay as "instructors" or "assessors" – reducing further their facility for professional judgment over adult learning.

"Many thought New Labour in 1997 would show a more benign attitude towards FE but those who did were proved wrong," suggested Birks. There was no return to local authority control, national pay bargaining or old conditions of service. Labour spent record resources on colleges, notably capital funds for new buildings and higher levels of grant, but with the money came increased levels of audit, league tables, performance targets and public "naming and shaming" of under-performing colleges. "New Labour shared almost the same objectives for FE as the Conservatives did before them. The only difference was that whereas the Conservatives thought service improvements could be achieved through market pressure, New Labour was more disposed to use planning and intervention, to 'top-slice' FE funds to secure improvements." So, a greater proportion of core funding was diverted into initiatives to lever change, such as the Teachers' Pay Initiative, Standards

Fund, Centres of Vocational Excellence, disastrous Individual Learning Accounts that collapsed in fraud, and learndirect.

The instrument for intervention was the Learning and Skills Council, replacing the Further Education Funding Council in 2000. The LSC was created as a strategic planning body, to which the colleges' own strategic plans would become subordinate. Local programmes for adults judged highly successful one week were sacrificed at the altar of new national policies and strategy the next. "What colleges wanted for learners was regarded as secondary or irrelevant against LSC statutory plans for meeting the needs of employers, skills shortages, etc," observed Birks. The taps for everything other than what the Government deemed necessary were being turned off.

Frustrations were voiced repeatedly by participants at all three conferences that politicians and policy makers imposed reform after reform without giving any one initiative time to become embedded. Four "Rs" had dominated two decades of reform – *Restructuring* colleges, *Redefining* adult learning entitlements, *Redirecting* cash to new targets and *Reshaping* college jobs to suit latest policy imperatives.

Consequences, intended or unintended, were increased managerial controls and bureaucracy, but reduced teacher autonomy, adult and community learning and scope for provision, as more of the resource was set aside to pay for private training.

In the end, no-one is satisfied

Another fundamental question that merged from partici-pants at the outset was: why are problems over workplace assessment so intractable now, when employers took control 20 years ago through NVQs? Why too did New

Labour fail in its early promise to tackle employers over their refusal to pay for adequate workplace training? Instead, the culture of blaming colleges for failing to meet employer demand continued. When colleges were confident they had identified need and were satisfying demand, once again they found themselves under orders to change. For example, South Birmingham, with the ethos of a community college, achieved excellent reports from the Adult Learning Inspectorate/Ofsted and local industry and commerce for recruiting under-achievers and hard-to-reach learners. "We had 58 per cent Level 1 and below," Birks reminded us. Then the ground rules changed and the LSC said concentrate on Level 2. "But there is an issue. If you want to engage people in learning, it is like asking them to climb a ladder with the bottom 12 rungs missing." It is around such areas that politicians will find many of the millions missing from adult learning, he said. Similarly in Liverpool, a successful city-wide community education scheme, aimed at Entry Level and Level 1, was wound-up despite overwhelming support for the SAFE (Save Adult Further Education) campaign.

There was considerable evidence of other unintended consequences of policy development. For example, for Robin Landman, chief executive of the Network for Black Professionals, said that few initiatives since the early 1990s have seriously addressed the needs of the Black and Minority Ethnic (BME) population. "Incorporation was an unmitigated disaster for black managers because principals could get rid of people they felt they had been obliged to employ," he said. And BME adults were ill-served by the domination of the skills agenda over wider questions of social justice. The statistics spoke for themselves, he added.

Pointing to a range of analyses, including work of the Government Actuary Department, Lifelong Learning UK and his own network research, Robin Landman indicated:

"Blacks are over-represented on training courses but under-represented when it comes to getting jobs. Forty per cent of the BME community in work-based learning get jobs as against with 70 per cent of whites. There is a lot more to do engaging with employers." Despite recent developments requiring colleges and other providers to carry out race, gender and disability impact assessments, advancement was slow, particularly in the appointment of black people to senior posts.

The skills agenda could not tackle the wider issues of discrimination, he said, where black people were over-represented in prisons and among under-achievers, faced increasing competition from white migrants, were excluded from many employment opportunities and lacked role models. "We must address black learner under-achievement in a sophisticated way. Don't just go for Leitch but Leitch-plus – skills and social justice in equal measure."

Many participants, supporting this view, said there was evidence that the Government's employer demand-led policies had become a major obstacle to progress. Ruth Serwotka, head of equality and diversity at South London Learning and Skills Council, said: "Demand-led actually means giving rather a lot of money to employers. This is not the best way to ensure that discrimination does not take place. If funding is going through employers, it will be spent on the people who have got jobs, which is disproportionately *not* minority groups."

Yet, even with demand-led policies coming on train, employers still seem far from content. As we see later in this report, there have been wider frustrations around issues of assessment and qualifications, with a culture clash between what employers believe they should pay for and the wider education many adults and providers believe should be an entitlement. And the FE workforce is itself part of the bigger picture. David Hunter, chief executive of LLUK, the sector skills council for all staff in post-16 learning, pointed out that the key question was how to retrain staff to get right the balance between the economy and wider community. "Whatever the future, there is a need for a well-trained workforce."

As a precursor to the Government's pending review of adult learning, John Denham, Secretary of State for DIUS, said evidence from his Department suggested the need for a radical rethink about how we provide adult learning in the age of Information and Learning Technology and the new opportunities for distance learning it creates. Although ILT is a useful tool, there was concern that it is not a panacea and that over-reliance on this method would lose the all-important social context of learning.

Susan Pember, director of FE, learning and skills at DIUS, made it clear that for the foreseeable future, "Leitch is the blueprint". Independent machinery – including the Commission on Employment and Skills and National Learner Panel – was in place to keep the Government up to the mark on its plans. "By 2011, £900m would be spent on Train to Gain, but that still leaves £2bn for other routes and Learner Accounts (since re-labelled Skills Accounts)." Other necessary reforms would include a strong adult information, advice and guidance (IAG) service. "The individual trainee must have really good advice before they commit themselves to a programme because they will be paying up to 50 per cent of the fee."

But was this really a new revolution or just another round of initiatives, to be superseded by something else in the none-too-distant future?

CHAPTER 2

FIVE CONUNDRUMS

Where are we today with adult learning? What is its prime purpose? Indeed, can such a function be clearly defined? As we have seen in the preceding chapter, the past 20 years have seen repeated and failed struggles by successive governments to strike a balance between learning for work – for the improvement of skills for the economy – and for leisure, including academic, pursuits. At every turn, armies of existing and potential learners fall victim to the unintended consequences of policy change. This time, with the latest strategic developments based on the Leitch and Foster reports, ministers accepted as a price worth paying the loss of perhaps 500,000 adults to the system which focused on "other" adult learning. In the event, more than a million lost out and, as was amply demonstrated at the series of NIACE conferences, new legions of "nearly poor" are emerging. These are the adults deemed too wealthy for fee remission or other subsidies/benefits and too poor to afford the fees. They are also substantially people who cannot benefit or are not yet ready for the Leitch-Foster agenda. As we explore these and other issues, the conundrums around latest policy developments raise a number of key questions:

- What is learning for?
- Who are FE institutions for?
- How do we create meaningful adult qualifications?
- What about the workers?
- And who pays?

What is learning for?

Lynne Sedgmore, chief executive of the Centre for Excellence in Leadership, has lived through many 'eras' in FE – the technical era, franchise era, community college era and skills era. Throughout, there been a false dichotomy in thinking at policy level, she said. "There was always an assumption that we cannot have excellence *and* social cohesion; that we must choose between skills *or* recreational, vocational *or* liberal education, robots *or* fully-rounded human beings, economic growth or social cohesion, competition *or* collaboration."

But she was inspired by David Blunkett's vision of the Learning Age in 1998 when he called for the "development of creativity with learning valued for its own sake as a key contributor in creating a civilised society, healthy communities and a flourishing economy," and spoke of learning "developing the spiritual side of our lives," and "nourishing our souls."

This view envisaged every adult as a learner, including education practitioners, "leaders who should become role models of reflective, learning practitioners for their students." It called for an overarching, joined-up vision of adult education that includes priorities from all government departments – DIUS, the Department of Communities and Local Government, Department of Work and Pensions and the Department of Culture and Sport, she said.

Dan Taubman, senior national education officer for the Universities and Colleges Union, built on this vision with the concept of a comprehensive FE system "working for equality and inclusion and serving all its surrounding communities". It should support lifelong learning and be based in the public sector but working with other organisations such as schools, local government and the voluntary sector to support neighbourhood and civic renewal, as well as economic development.

A central message from conference participants was that good quality education should be focused on the learner rather than a policy. Caroline Gray, Curriculum Manager,

City College, Birmingham, called for "a service that is there when you need it, not a narrow package given to you when someone else needs it." The message from FE should be, "Come to us and we will meet your needs, not wait until you fit certain criteria." Gemma Tumelty, president of the National Union of Students, agreed but asked, "Who is listening to the learners? They will know what learning is for." (See case study, page 19.)

True education is a gradual and profound process of acquiring knowledge and skills, a drawing-out of potential and talent, said Maire Daley, chair of the UCU's education committee. Neil Scales, director general of Merseytravel, echoed this, describing how some of his employees had overcome years of poor self-image through adult education. Bobby learned to use computers to keep up with his grandchildren and can look forward to a retirement full of interest, he said, while Linda overcame her fear of Maths to achieve a full Level 2 IT qualification. "We need learning that empowers the individual and the employer. How difficult can it be?" he asks. (See Merseylearn case study, page 21.)

Maire Daley contrasted this empowering interpretation of education with Professor. Frank Coffield's bleak definition of employability as no more than "a readiness to be trained and retrained whatever types of employment are available, leaving students searching for solutions to systemic problems."

And there was a timely reminder from Tony Benn, former government minister, that throughout history governments tried to control education, defining what sort of things could be "known" by different groups of people. "In the fifteenth century people were burned for reading the Bible and in the 1700s, they had been imprisoned for reporting debates in the House of Commons," he said. "The 1870 Education Act had been about preparing people for industry while the 1944 Education Act had tried to classify people permanently into different types of mind for different occupations at the age of eleven."

But in a democracy people have the power to vote, he said, and they need education to use it well. Using technology, for example, needs not only technical knowledge but also the ability to think morally and politically about how it should be used and what our priorities are. He was reminded of a letter from a constituent admiring the landing of the Moon vehicle but wondering why the Bristol bus service couldn't be sorted out.

"Education encourages people to come out ten feet tall – and if you do that, many of these problems we talk about today can be solved," he concluded. "Only a nation that is able to continue education through adult life can resolve problems."

What is the role of FE institutions?

As we saw in Chapter 1, under incorporation colleges were removed from Local Authority control and established as independent institutions run by business people, in the hope that competition would drive up standards by eliminating poor provision. Then the LSC was created, as a strategic planning body, and colleges became answerable to it for government planning and targets through Grant Letters and Public Service Agreements.

Self-regulation and the reform of the LSC will alter the position again, but Alan Birks, former Principal of South Birmingham College, showed how that relationship will be far from clear. The Governing Board is responsible for the nature and strategy of the college, for staff pay and conditions and industrial relations, but the LSC will be able to replace the Principal and appoint and dismiss governors.

The lesson of history is that colleges are pulled in many directions by different paymasters and policy-makers. How, then, can the sector make sure that the needs of individuals and the community are heard? With the creation of two government departments and the swing back to "localism", the LSC loses 70 per cent of its funds to local authorities for the under-19s and will no longer be the main funder of some colleges. This situation is welcomed by Paul Head, Principal of the College of North East London (CONEL), who will be looking for funding from other government departments and agencies, such as the health service, as well as the private sector. It should chime with Lynne Sedgmore's call for overarching joined-up government.

He also expects to collaborate with other providers. "No institution can provide all services, so there will need to be area planning and co-operation. And if the whole community is to be served, colleges will need to retain a sense of public ethos," he maintained.

Getting meaningful adult qualifications

Is it possible to have a qualifications framework that satisfies the needs of both employers and individual learners? Contradictory evidence of what individuals needed and what employers said they could afford emerged repeatedly throughout the conferences.

There was general agreement that building up units to form a qualification was a practical idea. The challenge was, however, to select units that were relevant to employers' needs but also made a coherent package for the learner, enabling them to make progress in their learning and careers. Judith Swift, development manager for unionlearn, argued that "The qualifications will need to be portable, recognisable and useful – and in the employees' pocket, not on the employers' wall." (See unionlearn case study, page 22.)

Even so, were this challenge met, a big question remains around how to meet the needs of those not in the workforce – a dilemma that has dogged efforts to provide and accredit ESOL (see case study, page 24).

Then there is the proliferation of qualifications that successive governments have pledged and failed to tackle for decades. The current "spaghetti" of qualifications is a meal that pleases no-one. Employers do not understand its complexity and many still think in terms of certificates that have not been awarded for many years.

Brian Wisdom, chief executive of People 1st (the Sector Skills Council for hospitality, leisure, travel and tourism), said that of the current workforce of two million, 750,000 will need training to reach the appropriate Level 2 and 3 skills requirements. Two-thirds of employers are training, but only 3 per cent of that training resulted in a recognised qualification – and with nearly 300 sector specific qualifications, there is a desperate need for rationalisation of the Qualifications and Curriculum Framework.

The SSCs representing employers are now in control of reforming vocational qualifications. They want small units, saying that the "full-fat" Level 2 takes too long to achieve. As an example, People 1st is working with lecturers and awarding bodies on an entry qualification for chefs that will consist of 12 mandatory units and a practical test, a fit-for-purpose apprenticeship and a more flexible system of unitisation for training for those who are in work.

But is it possible to create a simple and straightforward package that will meet the needs of a variety of employers? Can People 1st, for instance, design entry qualifications and further units for chefs that will satisfy hotel and restaurant chains as well as smaller independent restaurants and the corner café?

There is also need for agreement on who pays for which aspects of training. Brian Wisdom wants a re-balancing of employer-led demands and the demands of public service agreement targets in Train to Gain.

What about the workers?

The Government is calling for a world-class FE workforce to train Britain's workers in the skills they need for a competitive economy. All teachers will have to be trained, or working toward a qualification, by 2010 and undertake CPD to maintain their licence to practice as members of the Institute for Learning. By 2012 all new principals or those moving posts should be qualified.

The Government wants high quality and value for money. But since incorporation, value for money has often meant a casualised workforce that can be taken on or laid off at will, as numerous reports to the conferences revealed. Career paths have been distorted as jobs increasingly become short-term contracts with responsibilities defined by temporary projects and funding streams. Contact hours have increased and holidays reduced, making CPD difficult. Teaching quality has increasingly been judged by mechanistic and inflexible criteria.

In the face of these difficulties, Lifelong Learning UK, the Sector Skills Council for the sector, is responsible for professionalising the workforce and is currently working on new qualifications and CPD requirements. David Hunter, its chief executive, told conference participants that he saw the need for greater planning in the future, based on detailed labour market information about the needs of the FE workforce. Other priorities were to attract and retain the best people, improve the sector's image and ensure that equality and diversity were at the heart of policy-making, strategy, planning and training.

The UCU is optimistic that developing the existing workforce, or growing your own, could be a good way of promoting equality and diversity. And Christine Lewis, Unison national officer, also reminded the conference that the majority of the workforce in FE were not teachers and that their needs had also to be addressed for the benefit of the learners and the morale of the workforce.

However, considerable concern was expressed by participants over the vulnerable state of continuing professional development, despite new regulations in place to secure it. Paul Head warned that the funding for training "does not stack up" and that in hard times the CPD budget was the easiest to cut. He also stated his belief that FE needs to find a way for staff to make themselves heard on training matters without it becoming an industrial relations issue. But Maire Daley pointed out that where there is not sufficient training and support for the workforce, industrial relations can be the only forum in which the value of the staff is discussed.

Who pays?

With one million adults lost to adult learning, as funding is diverted into skills training – a trend that looks set to continue – the question of who pays, is paramount. Everyone accepted that costs had to be shared between the state, employer and individual. However, there was considerable evidence at the conferences of skewing essential resources away from those in greatest need.

Paul Head showed the conference some projected figures for London which indicate that spending on full Levels 2 and 3, Skills for Life, Foundation Learning Tier and ESOL will flatline or rise slightly while "all other" adult education spending plummets from £120 million to £17 million by 2010.

The spending is there, says Christine Lewis, but it is going into training. What no-one knows is whether the people who were in adult education are now being trained or whether they have disappeared from the system. Leisha Fullick, Pro-Director (London) at the Institute of Education, chairing the second conference, pointed out that it had been impossible to find out but, as participants agreed, research had to be carried out.

Many speakers supported the view that social justice should be about helping people into employment and up the ladder into better, sustainable jobs, and that priority should be given to those who missed out on earlier education and need a second chance.

But channelling the money through employers for skills concentrates on those already in employment and further marginalises the minority groups who are least likely to have jobs. It also does nothing for those people who do not have the confidence to re-engage with learning. They need 'toe-in-the-water' courses that are inviting, non-threatening and do not have assessment demands hanging over them to remind them of the times when they have failed academically before. Concentrating funding on what could be described as narrow, utilitarian courses will not serve the most excluded and needy.

Colleges are also expected to increase fees in future: up to 50 per cent of the cost of the course. While there was agreement that those who could pay should pay, fee increases will hit a new group of the low-paid known as the 'nearly poor.' They will not be able to afford the fees but they will not be able to claim subsidies either because they are not unemployed or on benefits (see case study, page 25).

Jon Gamble, director for Adults and Lifelong Learning at the LSC, told the conference that he was struck by the complex agenda that everyone in the sector faces. While formal learning and skills will remain at the top of the list, he said that the LSC would like to see a broader offer and that "formulas and systems have their limits."

"You can't determine the priority status of learners simply by Skills for Life or Level 1 and 2 provision. That's right for the majority but many people have priorities not impacted by public service agreements and targets. We want to support sub-Level 2 learning and those with learning disabilities and those who want to learn for wider benefit," he said.

The collapse of a highly successful community education scheme in Liverpool following £5m cuts in funding served to amplify this issue. (See case study, page 26.)

CASE STUDIES

1) The learner voice?

Colleges would gain a powerful extra voice in support of better funding for adult education if they gave the learners more representation and influence over decision-making, said Gemma Tumelty, President of the National Union of Students.

In universities, students of higher education controlled vast budgets allowing them to set up effective systems to support students and voice their concerns, questions and complaints about their education. This in itself was a powerful educational tool.

But, in FE, amounts spent on student representation were tiny, with damaging results, she said. "The representation, advocacy and complaints regime for the 'clients' in FE in comparison with schools, universities, the NHS, the railways – almost every other public or quasi-public service – is just about the worst in the UK."

Drawing on recent NUS research evidence, she said colleges paid students little more than lip-service. "College websites talk about that adult environment, prospectuses, leaflets and open evenings. But is it true? Our members are attracted to and motivated by the adult brand, but the reality is that FE's 'Adult Environment' is partly mythological. They tell us that it is equally and as often conservative, paternalistic and run in the interests not of learners but of colleges as providers, who market but do not deliver that expected adult environment."

Everyone, from the governing bodies to tutors able to initiate or resist change, needed to take action. Despite a legal requirement on colleges to draw up and monitor a Learner Engagement Strategy, NUS continued to hear the "usual excuses" from colleges. They suggested "student apathy" was to blame when representative recruitment drives failed, rather than lack of money to promote them. Colleges often they said they could not fund unions properly since "things are different in FE". Others said learner-governor posts failed because students were "intimidated by white middle-class men in suits".

"But our research demonstrates that with board and senior management buy-in, backing from enthusiastic staff given time to do it, and a modest level of funding – as well as clear support for a development plan – student representation can survive and flourish."

She called for five steps to change attitudes: full training courses for student representatives, a proper channel for hearing and acting on student comments, serious discussions about student union budgets – not a social club for young A-level students but a representative body – professional staff support to co-ordinate representation across the college, and the development of a student organisation "within the ethos of the college".

"Sadly I still hear the view promoted that Student Evaluations are worthless – that we can learn nothing from their views and that we should all do our best to resist them, she said. "Adults in FE – the very people we need to engage most in education – don't need a student association that organises a disco once a term. They need their voice encouraged, funded and supported, both collectively and individually."

2) How difficult can it be?

The skills push is not for everyone, said a leading employer in the North West who has called for urgent steps to protect funding for the full range of learning programmes and prevent the exclusion of adults with greatest need.

Neil Scales, director general of Merseytravel, runs one of the most successful employer-driven adult learning programmes in the UK. Launched four years ago, Merseylearn is open to all 924 employees, from the cleaners to directors, in a company that manages the transport network for Merseyside, including the Mersey Tunnel.

Since its launch, more than nine out of ten employees have a level 2 qualification with a high proportion progressing to higher levels. Moreover, employee relations and retention rates have improved dramatically with a corresponding fall in grievances. Sick leave dropped by an average two days a week, equal to a saving of £150,000 a year, and customer complaints have fallen by half.

However, success depended on sustaining high levels of funding for all types of provision, not just those for employability, he said. He accepted that funding had to be prioritised around Train to Gain, Apprenticeships and basic skills, with fees for those who could afford to pay. But much of the commercial success was attributable to satisfaction arising from success in courses such as IT for leisure, languages, photography and aromatherapy.

"These are learners who would never in a million years set foot inside an FE college. For many learners, however friendly these may be, they still have too many memories of school. However, through the learning centres, adult education provision and tutors, learndirect provision and the work of unionlearn reps, we are getting more and more learners back into education."

Merseylearn began under the banner of "community education" with full funding but increasingly depends on help from partners to support learning of this type. The question was how to support those staff with who often earned the least, but had most need to return to learning. "If we charged for all courses, those who could pay would, but we could well lose those who most needed or who would benefit from the learning. Embedding skills for life worked for some programmes but not all. If Merseytravel paid for everything we ran the risk, as a public sector organisation, of being accused of wasting public money.

"We decided the way forward was to develop a collective learning fund, which will offer another way, through the financial support of ourselves as an employer and the trade unions and its members, the opportunity to fund and loan money for programmes that are not vocationally focused, whether it is at a Merseylearn centre or through signposting to another provider. How difficult can it be?"

3) Unionlearn – an essential partnership with FE
Unionlearn representatives have found that adult learners want more than they are offered and this is far wider than a diet of skills for work. For example, gardeners at a mental health institution were offered more horticulture studies by their employers, when what they really wanted, they told them, was education for better understanding of the issues facing the patients they talked to every day. In another scheme, school caretakers were found to bond better with children when they became learners themselves. Judith

Swift, development manager for unionlearn, said, "We need to think through the business case for wider learning because it goes beyond the skills agenda."

The roots of unionlearn reach back to 1992 and the creation of a new style of learning rep for the workplace, working in partnership with employers. Now, more than 250,000 employees pass through unionlearn programmes each year. Unison alone has 3,000 reps, 80 learning agreements with colleges and 10,000 members currently on courses. Every year, 45 per cent progress on from Level 2 to Level 3 studies.

"Unionlearn reps and the FE system work together; they need each other," says Judith Swift. "Huge numbers of them are trained by people in FE." Any loss of FE tutors and support staff, with the switch from "other" adult learning to skills training and a greater focus on instructors could prove detrimental.

The pursuit of a skills-plus agenda resulted, she said, in democratic and more equal workplaces, confident people, better industrial relations, healthier and safer workplaces and better-trained staff. "But, to achieve this, we need stability of FE provision, union aware staff, a partnership approach and a well-paid and trained workforce.

"Learning has to be for the benefit of employees as well as employers – not necessarily the same thing. Workforce learners are aspirational; they want a bit of all kinds of learning. First steps are important but very often, people who start bite-size need the full meal and we have to make sure they get it. Full fat must be as fat as it needs to be for these individuals. Qualifications need to be in the employees' pockets, not on the employers' walls."

"Workplace cohesion is not on a different planet from social cohesion – families and workplace are part of the same picture."

4) ESOL

Nowhere is the damage of unintended consequences more apparent than in the provision of English for speakers of other languages (ESOL). What appeared to be a generous initial allocation of resources and professional discretion was soon outstripped by demand from a rapidly rising migrant workforce alongside more than expected growth in domestic demand. Jon Gamble, LSC director for Adults and Lifelong Learning, said that when the LSC reviewed uptake, it found "a large amount of unmet demand, while some individuals were moving between providers on different days, so getting a lot more than others". Subsequent changes in "learning products" for ESOL and the way funding was allocated meant we were actually able to increase the impact," he insisted. "There will be groups and individuals who cannot afford to pay and we need to look at how to support them."

However, evidence to the Universities and Colleges Union from teachers and students showed that enrolments had been badly affected and people were being turned away in far larger numbers than government ministers expected when they sanctioned the changes. John Denham, Education Secretary, said this would be studied in the Government's review of adult learning. Maire Daley, UCU's education committee chair, told conference participants: "The most affected are beginners and Entry Level participants, particularly women and people on low incomes. The Department has had a go at the issue of ESOL access, using hardship funds but it is not working well and it is temporary." Ministers had done a U-turn on proposed funding, particularly for London, but still demanded a switch to work-related learning. Alan Tuckett, chairing the third conference, reported that NIACE had detected similar issues to those raised by the UCU with this shift of resources. "The key poorest groups in Britain are least likely to be in the labour market. What are we doing for them, for example, Pakistani women?"

Dan Taubman, UCU senior education official, pointed to a deeper, longer-term issue of staff cuts following changes in funding priorities for ESOL. "We charge fees for ESOL, then essential provision is cut because of the changing priorities and the fact that they are no longer part of the important targets. This point was amplified by Paul Head, principal of CONEL, who said funding for ESOL, along with other basic skills provision, was "flat-lining or going up a bit" for the foreseeable future. He doubted whether there would be enough to meet demand and warned that staffing issues had to be considered. An overwhelming concern expressed by the conference was whether sufficient ESOL staff would remain in the FE system.

5) Funding failures

A new educational underclass is emerging from the unintended consequences of Government policies to promote skills. This group, described as the 'nearly poor', includes hundreds of thousands of adults just above the breadline but lacking any entitlement to welfare benefits or support with college fees.

Such groups were at the centre of almost every case study discussed at the three conferences. For example, Peter Davies, principal of the City Lit in London, comes into contact with them every working day and described the "near impossible challenge" of trying to engineer what the college delivers into the neat boxes demanded by bureaucrats who turn up to check that everything "fits" the Government's new skills agenda.

A typical example of courses currently undermined by current policy was the craft of "bookbinding" It ticked all the right boxes for programme progression, PCDL, social justice and fairness. "But how do you define that field of learning?" Without carrying a qualification – which the learners neither need nor want – that fits a specific set of skills on the LSC list, it would not qualify for subsidy.

"When we asked what they wanted from the course, one was retired and wanted to look after his books, two were self-employed, one worked in a small museum and could not afford the fees, one said simply 'learning is good for you'."

"If people can afford to pay the fees, all well and good. Two people there with lots of books might well have been able to afford it. But how do we know? Remember that the NHS tried means-testing and it did not work. If you are the working poor, you are going to be excluded from the market. How do we include such people if we have no flexibility, no movement?"

6) Liverpool – Save Adult Further Education
"In Liverpool, £5m has been lost to adult learning over the past few years, so it is impossible not to conclude that there must be fewer adults being given opportunities. Teachers have gone, courses have gone, students have gone."

In saying this, Maire Daley, chair of the University and College Union education committee, was mindful of the benefits new skills-based learning opportunities had been generated post-Leitch. But at what cost? A community-based adult learning programme of proven worth, praised by Ofsted for reaching the hard-to-reach, closed when national policy meant funding was switched from "other" adult learning to skills for employability.

It was a comprehensive programme including Entry Level, Level 1 and Level 2 in a broad-based community programme based on individual needs. "The teaching and learning focused on personal skills within the community and for employment – offering a whole range of avenues to success, where and when the adults needed them."

Staff and managers with years of community education experience had in their professional judgment worked out how best to help these people onto a range of learning ladders, including those for skills. "That programme doesn't exist anymore in the new system of funding," comented Daley.

The funding tap was turned off, despite a spirited SAFE – Save Adult Further Education – campaign, backed by the local Labour MP Louise Ellman, a petition to 10 Downing Street signed by thousands and a wealth of evidence on the campaign website of the way the learning had changed people's lives.

"The campaign, started by practitioners and students, challenged the idea that the funding shift would lead to new provision by taking out the community-based route. Indeed, many of the opportunities that have arisen are taken by people already in jobs."

CHAPTER 3

CONFERENCE RECOMMENDATIONS

Participants at the conferences called for adult learning to be given due recognition, funding and status through a clear set of policies and entitlements – extending the principles behind Every Child Matters to the equally big idea that Every Adult Matters. This, they said, needs a serious attempt to work out a clear philosophy and sustainable set of strategies for adult learning which develops and nurtures self-confidence, breaks down social and economic barriers, promotes social cohesion and helps transform lives – creating critical, active citizens. This was the way to develop the educated, flexible, creative adults "required" for the 21st century.

While the importance of education and training for employability and professional enhancement was understood, there was a general feeling that too much money went into Train to Gain, with too much emphasis on the employers' agenda, to the detriment of funding for general adult earning with reasonable individual choice of courses. This was seen as particularly important for older and retired people, the emerging excluded "nearly poor" and others marginalised as an unintended consequence of constant changes in Government policy, all of whom could be helped through adult learning to maintain simulating independent lives.

To achieve the goals for adult learning, they agreed, it was essential to adopt, cherish and fight for some things and avoid, ditch or resist others:

What is learning for?

What to adopt, cherish and fight for
- Preserve and value adult learning and skills – formal and informal – across a broad curriculum
- Cherish the values of adult education – access for all, voluntary access and self-selection, inclusiveness, the process of learning and additional "unrecorded" benefits of learning
- Maintain social justice and value progression
- Value those things which adult learners bring to learning
- Recognise opportunities for adults beyond skills-based learning, including the huge benefits in personal development and health and well-being for individuals
- Recognise the "skills" inherent in adult and community learning that are often under-funded
- Keep the emphasis on "education", not just training, while recognising the importance of training for employability, work and enhancement
- Value "first", "second" and "third" chance education
- Keep trade union education alive

What to avoid, ditch or resist
- Reject a narrow, mechanistic, skills-based perspective
- Do not re-invent the old tripartite secondary modern/technical/grammar system within colleges
- Do not lose education for education's sake – learning for just learning
- Ditch the acronyms that define learning (e.g. PCDL) and concentrate on working out with clarity the purposes of learning
- Do not distort the curriculum to match the funding
- End training as "assessment" not education
- Reject the idea that people are trained once for ever – eg. Longbridge

Who are the learners?

What to adopt, cherish and fight for
- Broaden the definition of "demand" to include the needs of individuals, not predominantly of employers
- Widen opportunities for 'ordinary' people to undertake programmes that enable them to fulfil their interests at a reasonable cost
- Cherish diversity of age range of learners
- Ensure equality of access, with more sensible consideration of issues such as the level of fees, state subsidies, ease of location, childcare, etc
- Do more to promote a positive approach to equality and diversity
- Provide better-supported learning at all levels for people with disabilities and mental health challenges

What to avoid, ditch or resist
- Avoid a system driven solely by employability and business
- Avoid social and economic exclusion – too many initiatives and funding policies result in this

What is the role of FE institutions?

What to adopt, cherish and fight for
- Develop FE colleges as a central service for the local community
- Ensure high-quality provision and more effective collaboration with partners
- Embrace change as a "two-way process" between government and FE
- Value plumbing and pilates
- Listen to the voice of the learner

- Nurture informal education and community learning
- Maintain different kinds of delivery sites (colleges, schools, community centres, workplace, and so on) from first steps learning onwards to meet individual needs and remove barriers to learning
- Be a voice for the disenfranchised and marginalised
- Return to the widening participation agenda
- Create what John Denham, Secretary of State, called "wriggle room" for more flexibility to provide "other" adult learning
- Give greater recognition to the valuable work done by Local Authorities and the voluntary sector in adult and community education

What to avoid, ditch or resist

- Stop following fads, fashions and short-term initiatives – staff, colleges, learners and their communities need stability to flourish
- Guard against the rise of pointless bureaucracy and paperwork
- Stop the constant and unnecessary organisational change
- Prevent the loss of adult education environment (for example, from having too many pre-16s in college)
- Avoid repeating past mistakes – Individual Learning Accounts, Connexions cards and so on
- Resist the exclusive dominance of big colleges
- Review the role of Ofsted and whether it is suitable for colleges
- Ditch the financially wasteful and unnecessarily complex quangos in the FE system
- End the costly and unnecessary brokerage system around employment-related training
- Avoid over-restrictive, inflexible policies
- Resist over-dominance of prescriptive inspection and audit regimes

Getting meaningful qualifications

What to adopt, cherish and fight for
- Non-accredited learning as first steps back into learning
- Maintain the steps to learning
- Make accreditation sensitive and relevant to individual needs
- Restore the intermediate steps to progression that have disappeared
- Base learning on credits and units that individuals and employers want. Full-fat Level 2 as a target is too rigid
- Allow students more time to build confidence and gain underpinning skills before embarking on an accredited course
- Create specialised diplomas and credit based courses for adults

What to avoid, ditch or resist
- End the obsession with qualifications rather than out-comes
- Prevent domination of learning by large qualifications – more bite-size qualifications are required
- End the crude way progression is used to measure the value of a course – especially for students with disabilities
- Remove barriers to access such as entry requirements, blunt and unsophisticated achievement recording as success measures

Further Education workforce

What to adopt, cherish and fight for
- Value and build on the diversity, quality and commitment of the adult learning workforce in adult and community learning and colleges
- Funding for initial FE teacher training should be on a par with that for school teachers

- Ensure CPD for all staff – not just teachers
- Create an industrial relations environment that sees full implementation of national agreements
- Restore trust in expertise of professionals to define what is a successful outcome
- Fight to retain a workforce that is duly rewarded, with better conditions of service
- Create more permanent teaching posts
- Create space and time for lecturers to really prepare good lessons and discuss the issues

What to avoid, ditch or resist
- Casualisation, low wages, poor conditions and poor contracts
- Long-hours culture
- Lack of staff training

Funding

What to adopt, cherish and fight for
- Create financial incentives for collaboration in FE that include voluntary and community sectors
- Finance robust plans for sustainability
- Fund learning by credits and units to help move people towards their learning goals
- Improve education maintenance allowances and a dditional learning support fund
- Guarantee the right to education with financial support beyond basic skills and Level 1 courses
- Adopt a national funding methodology framework for staff pay and conditions
- Ensure longer-term funding guarantees for colleges and other providers in order to bring stability
- Recognise the need for the state, employer and individual to invest in learning and skills
- Make funding arrangements transparent
- Fight for full adult funding entitlement to Level 3

What to avoid, ditch or resist

- Resist higher fees, since these deter learners
- Reduce the emphasis on competition through contestability
- Avoid "spurts" of funding which do not meet needs
- Eliminate transitory and short-term project funding which is not sustainable and funding regimes that eliminate choice
- End inequalities in funding and funding formulae
- Stop privatising the FE system
- Take measures against employers who shun their financial responsibility for staff training
- End the 16-hour rule (benefits trap)
- Avoid funding provision without some learning aims
- Do not restrict Additional Learning Support to accredited learning

How it can be done

What to adopt, cherish and fight for

- Have more campaigns such as that fought over ESOL
- Support and fund the Foundation Learning Tier, Entry Level and Level 1 provision as essential first steps of a learning pathway
- Cherish diversity of the FE system – local providers providing for the local community along the lines of community colleges
- Improve all channels of communication
- Preserve the personal and community development learning (PCDL) safeguard for non-vocational courses
- Improve Train to Gain
- Improve adult information, advice and guidance – a hastily thrown-together service will be a waste of money
- Give more support for taster-courses to get new and reluctant learners engaged

What to avoid, ditch or resist

- Resist the total focus on hitting Government targets
- End mechanistic approach to education
- Do not look at the past through rose-tinted glasses
- Ditch brokerage services that are inappropriate and do not deliver

APPENDIX I

The Conference Speakers

Learning from the Past Decade (1997-2007): what to adopt and what to avoid – Thursday 8 November 2007

Chair: Paul Mackney, Associate Director (FE) – NIACE

- Susan Pember, Director – FE, Learning & Skills Performance Group, DIUS
- Caroline Gray, UCU NEC, City College Birmingham
- Kat Fletcher, Centre for Excellence and Leadership (NUS President 2004-2006)
- Robin Landman, Chief Executive – Network for Black Professionals
- Alan Birks CBE, former Principal – South Birmingham College
- David Hunter, Chief Executive – Lifelong Learning UK

The Present (2007-2008): what to cherish and what to ditch – Thursday 29 November 2007

Chair: Leisha Fullick, Pro-Director (London) – Institute of Education

- Jon Gamble, LSC Director for Adults and Lifelong Learning
- Ellie Russell, NUS FE Officer 2005-07
- Christina McAnea, National Secretary for Education – UNISON
- Maire Daley, Chair – UCU Education Committee
- Paul Head, Principal College of North East London
- Brian Wisdom, CEO People First Sector Skills Council

**Preparing for the Future (2008-2015): what to
fight for and what to resist** – Thursday 17 January 2008

Chair: Alan Tuckett, Director – NIACE

- John Denham, Secretary of State – DIUS
- Dan Taubman, UCU National Head of FE
- Gemma Tumelty, President – NUS
- Judith Swift, TUC Unionlearn
- Lynne Sedgmore CBE, Chief Executive – Centre for
  Excellence in Leadership
- Neil Scales, Director General – MerseyTravel
- Tony Benn, former MP and government minister

APPENDIX 2

Government consultation on informal learning

The following is a combination of John Denham's speeches to NIACE on January 17 and to the Social Market Foundation on January 15 – on the launch of his inquiry into adult learning

The Department for Innovation, Universities and Skills was created by Gordon Brown on his first full day as Prime Minister. It brings together for the first time in government those strands of policy that are key to Britain's long-term economic and social well-being.

- Making the most of the skills of all our people.
- Producing world-class research and scholarship.
- Combining those skills and that research to create competitive businesses and innovative public services.
- And building a society where no-one is left behind, and where everyone can participate – thanks to higher wages, greater aspirations, or more secure and fulfilling lives.

These aims are precisely what DIUS is working towards. It means that we and our partners are at the centre of determining what kind of society we live in and what sort of country Britain can become. For this we need our education system to:

- respond to the needs of learners and employers
- provide level 2 training for all adults and
- secure the future of informal adult learning.

While the social dimension of the overall vision is important, it is a vision that is ultimately focused on economic activities and interests.

The twin purposes of adult education

The purpose of adult education has always been two-fold. It is clearly about enabling people to develop the skills and qualifications necessary to get better jobs. But it's also about meeting the basic human desire for intellectual stimulation and enlightenment. It's about adults building social bonds by sharing their interests and passions.

Indeed, it may be unrealistic to make a hard and fast distinction between these two functions. It's never easy to separate the practical benefits of learning from the accompanying sense of personal reward. Nowhere is this clearer than among adult learners below Level 2.

Learners with the determination to improve their basic skills not only make themselves more employable, but also find their aspirations and self-esteem rise at the same time. It is for both these reasons that we're spending £1.5 billion per annum on first-steps learning over three years. That total includes some £600 million on adult basic skills, around £300 million on English language teaching and £25 million on family learning.

Still, government does have to make some practical policy decisions. It is no secret that this Government has concentrated public money on improving skills and qualification levels across the workforce. Altogether, Government funding for post-16 learning and skills has increased from £6.5 billion per annum in 2001-02 to £11.2 billion in 2007-08. By 2010-11, it will be £12.5 billion – a doubling of investment over the course of a decade.

I make no apology for this. Teaching millions of people to read and write, helping more people find jobs and develop their careers is far from a narrow agenda. Those providers who aren't prepared to change with the times will lose funding to those who do, to those who give training when and where it is needed and we have begun the process of legislation for that.

This comes not from politicians but from society. We have to make sure that people who cannot participate in the global economy aren't left behind. It is crucial that we offer skills to people who face the greatest disadvantage.

In his report last year, Lord Leitch concluded – and the Government accepted – that by 2020, we will need to help two and a quarter million adults achieve functional competence in literacy, language and numeracy. And by 2010, we need to help over three million adults achieve their first full Level 2 qualification.

I want to open up a debate about another, complementary area of my Department's work. One that also has a vital role to play in shaping our country. I'm not defensive about acknowledging that our decision to prioritise formal education is one of the drivers for the current debate on informal adult learning. For we continue to recognise the enormous value of learning that is part-time, often un-structured and for which gaining qualifications is not the main purpose.

It's why DIUS is funding informal adult learning through a safeguarded budget of £210m each year during the comprehensive spending review period. It's why we allocate £15 million each year to trade union learning and provide core funding for NIACE.

The "quiet revolution" in informal learning

But the principal driver behind the launch of our consultations on the future of informal adult learning is the desire to ensure that our emphasis on vocational skills does not compromise the diverse and vibrant world of informal adult learning.

It also reflects the value we place on the long and rich history of adult education in this country. Trade unions, mechanics institutes, women's suffrage groups, political and religious groups, independent lending libraries – these were all part of the movement responsible for so many of today's universities, FE colleges and adult learning bodies. And organisations like the Workers' Educational Association and the Women's Institute remain very much part of the current learning landscape.

That landscape extends well beyond the influence of DIUS. Substantial support for adult learning also comes from other government departments – like Communities and Local Government – from the national lottery, from the private sector and from voluntary organisations.

For example, DCMS supports a huge range of learning opportunities through such bodies as the Arts Council, Sport England and the Museums, Libraries and Archives Council. The BBC continues to be a force for education as well as for information and entertainment. Museums and galleries, like Tate Modern, offer education services and facilities to growing numbers of visitors. Public libraries are at the forefront of community access to learning and information, and many are reinventing the services they offer.

I'm glad that my colleague James Purnell, who is directly responsible for all these institutions and services, is as excited about this consultation as I am. He shares my enthusiasm for a sector that has undergone such dramatic change, as people learn in different ways.

Some courses are still taught in the classroom at a fixed time – an approach that would have been clearly recognised 100 years ago. But adult learning may be as easily stimulated by a TV programme that prompts a trip to the local museum, or an internet search that leads to a group of like-minded learners.

Most strikingly, much of the innovation in this sector in the early 21st century has been driven and achieved by learners themselves. People adapting new technologies. Not relying on support from local or national government to organise activities, but seeking out fellow enthusiasts through online communities and other channels besides.

Much of this comes down to the lives people now lead. We are living longer and more healthily. More people are in work than ever before, including those past the traditional retirement age. We're increasingly mobile, both nationally and internationally.

Technology has undoubtedly shaped they way we now learn. But I think the changing patterns of learning reflect more profound changes in society. Across many aspects of public services and private activities, people are demanding a more personal approach. One that puts them in charge. One that gives them more say in what, how, where and when.

Informal adult learning is no different. People are choosing and creating new opportunities to learn for themselves. And where new opportunities open up, people are using them in new and sometimes unpredictable ways.

Our individual and collective interests in learning have thereby been enhanced. Around 80 per cent of adults in this country report that they're taking part in some form of learning. Two million people watch Open University programmes without necessarily signing up to a course.

3.4 million belong to the National Trust, which offers various learning options, many run by volunteers.

A further substantial section of the population participates in an estimated 50,000 books clubs. First Oprah, and then Richard and Judy have helped to shape this phenomenon, but the idea of bringing together people to discuss and to learn from literature comes from an earlier era. It lays at the heart of the adult education movement of the 19th and early 20th centuries, in places like the Swarthmore Settlement in Leeds, Ruskin College in Oxford and Toynbee Hall in London.

But what's different about the new ways of learning, is how people forge links between different activities, organisations and technologies. How a family visit to a museum can prompt explorations online or the decision to join a group of volunteers.

At a meeting last week, I heard about the growing enthusiasm for genealogy. Inspired by the success of *Who Do You Think You Are?*on BBC television, archives are full of people tracing their roots. People are turning to the web for online research tools and creating new history societies. They're even creating new community archives from scratch. And if we think for a moment about the wider benefits of family-tree planting, it can be the seed from which adults are inspired to improve their reading skills. It can be a springboard for further learning, a boost to self-confidence.

Why the consultation?
So now is an opportune time to consider how we can best support this vibrant culture of private and communal engagement – to investigate the causes and the outcomes of what amounts to a quiet learning revolution.

I have decided to take the lead in this process since DIUS and its predecessors have traditionally funded the greater part of education for adults as a whole – and it continues to make a significant contribution to informal learning.

I also want to challenge my department to respond to this story of tremendous dynamism, because DIUS is not just the department for colleges, universities and adult education services. It is also the department for students, for communities and for those adults who have yet had the chance to further their learning.

Equally, I want to challenge some of the recipients of DIUS funding – for, in truth, parts of the adult education sector have barely changed their approach in the past 50 years.

Much provision would be recognisable from Macmillan's day. It is isolated from the groundswell of popularly-organised learning, and it is missing out on the huge opportunities presented by technology.

The issues

So let me turn to the main questions and issues that we're keen to explore through the consultation.

Supporting learning from below

Our starting point must be mapping and quantifying the informal learning landscape. If we're to support people in taking control of their own learning, we must explore what's driving the range of activity that out's there, and understand how people move from one form of participation to another. How high-quality TV output inspires individuals to take an interest further, whether through the web or by seeking out similar enthusiasts locally.

The potential here for experts to share their passions on a voluntary basis is enormous, amply demonstrated by the

University of the Third Age. The U3A comprises 640 active groups involving almost 200,000 people and is entirely self-funded.

Similarly, the Young Foundation has been developing schoolofeverything.com – an online platform that allows learners and teachers to come together and organise their own learning activities. Already, it's offering topics as diverse as maths, yoga and blogging.

Indeed, the success of such ventures raises a serious question as to whether government needs to be involved in some voluntary activities at all.

The role of Government

But the role of Government in the broadest sense is an important part of this general debate – and here I mean all departments with a stake in informal learning, whose contributions need to be fully understood and recognised.

Now, given the diversity of need, demand and current activity, it strikes me that the creation of a single funding system or a centralised learning strategy is probably not the best way forward.

By contrast, if there are ways in which we can remove obstacles to the most cost-effective and productive use of resources, and introduce greater flexibility to funding streams, we absolutely want to hear what they are.

For example, that may involve offering easier access to public facilities, such as school buildings. There are already 8,000 extended schools, whose premises and modern ICT can be used for a plethora of community purposes. The same applies to Sure Start centres, Lottery-funded venues and the 6,000 UK online centres.

The adult education service

In the specific case of DIUS, we invite contributions on the future of adult education services themselves. What should be the future direction for a service that needs to transform itself in order to meet the demands of 21st-century learners?

I think there are several possibilities here in terms of prioritising use of the DIUS budget. We could continue giving subsidies to providers in order to arrange courses, or we could conclude that focusing spending on infrastructure might be a better use of money.

A further alternative could be to introduce real or virtual vouchers, a way of putting power in the hands of ordinary people, and enabling them to organise provision for their own learning. This idea could build on the mechanism being used for skills accounts from 2010.

Technology

If vouchers represent one kind of innovation, then it's vital that we harness the constant tide of advances in technology and broadcasting. Already RF chips are transforming our experience of museums, such that we can stand in front of a painting and enjoy commentary from leading art historians and curators. Mobile phones are now being used to guide tourists on walks through unfamiliar cities. Through the internet, new global communities have sprung up, bringing together people who suffer from specific medical conditions or are trying to learn the same language.

What's critical here is making the most of technology to facilitate learning, especially with the extension of broadband and the transition to digital television. The interactive possibilities in both spheres are considerable for learners, providers and government itself.

I'm delighted that a range of technology companies will be helping us with this work, including Sky, Microsoft, Intel and Vodafone. With their help and advice, I want the consultation to examine what future generations of learners might be able to do in the wake of further innovation. In what ways can we help people to better navigate often overwhelming amounts of information to identify the exactly the right learning opportunity for them? How can we help those who are isolated to participate in communal activities – a housebound person, say, who might communicate with book club companions through an interactive TV service?

Equality of access

Those two examples bring to me to the final major issue in the consultation. We recognise the fact that people from disadvantaged backgrounds stand to gain the most from learning, but that they often face the greatest barriers to doing so, whether through lack of money or mobility, because of learning difficulties or limited language skills.

We need to understand the barriers that currently exist – including the consequences of a digital divide – and how they affect particular sections of society.

But we must also guarantee equality of access to learning of all kinds. Ensuring that poorer people can access not only learning that's of practical use, but that satisfies their curiosities in the way it does for all.

This cannot be about separate provision for disadvantaged people. They have a right to exactly the same learning opportunities as those enjoyed by everyone else.

What now?

The last thing I'd like to cover this morning is the process for the consultation itself. It flows from our commitment to make DIUS a forward-thinking department in terms of working practices and its approach to policy creation that we want this consultation to be innovative and wide-ranging.

We want to hear from as many people as possible who are interested in adult learning. From learners themselves and from teachers, from small community groups and organisations of national breadth. We have already received valuable input from a wide range of sources – art galleries and archives, colleagues across government and bodies like NIACE.

I'm now delighted to announce that several important organisations have agreed to participate in five working groups addressing key areas of the consultation. These will cover technology, as I have explained, plus the voluntary sector, where the National Association for Voluntary and Community Action is signed up. A cross-government workstream, with support from the Office of the Third Sector and DCMS. A Families group, including the Family Learning Network. And an older people group, where U3A and Help the Aged will share their wisdom.

Together, we have a unique opportunity to ensure that informal education goes from strength to strength in the 21st century. This is our chance to build on the pioneering work of another era – of characters like Tawney and Toynbee, Cons and Birkbeck.

We should bear their legacy in mind during the weeks and months ahead – the spirit of innovation that drove those educators, trade unionists and public servants.

Where it currently exists, we should recognise, encourage and support that innovation. Where it could exist, we should create the conditions that will foster it.

To do so, we must reach out beyond existing institutions and providers – to hear from people and communities. How are their lives and needs changing? How do they wish to organise learning so that it is most useful and accessible to them? How do we build on the growing desire for people to come together and to organise their own learning?

Our vision for the future of informal learning must bring together and build on many interests; those of teachers and learners, communities and providers, traditions and technologies.

For my part, I'm looking forward to hearing your views. Thank you.

Other NIACE publications of interest

Eight in Ten: Adult learners in further education

The Report of the Independent Committee of Enquiry invited by the National Institute of Adult Continuing Education to review the state of adult learning in colleges of further education in England

Published by NIACE, 2005

ISBN 978 1 86201 278 3
Price £9.95

This Report argues for new thinking and new vocabulary in formulating policy and provision for adult learners. Chaired by Chris Hughes MBE, formerly Chief Executive of the Learning and Skills Development Agency, the Commission reflects on the need for a coherent strategy for lifelong learning. While accepting the need for a well-educated workforce, the Commission discusses the vital importance of a well-educated citizenry as well.

At the time of publication, eight in ten students in further education colleges in England were over the age of 19. Adults accounted for 50 per cent of taught hours in colleges. Yet adults seemed largely invisible in the concerns of politicians, policy-makers, heads of institutions and the press.

The Report reviewed the position of adult learners in further education, the longer-term implications of policy and skills strategies, trends in participation, the demand for adult learning in further education, successful initiatives in widening participation, and recommendations for further action.

Not Just the Economy: The public value of adult learning

Edited by Colin Flint and Chris Hughes

Published by NIACE, 2008

ISBN 978 1 86201 332 2
Price £12.95

Some 1.4 adults have been lost from state-funded educational provision since 2005. Government strategies have focused on the 16-19 age cohort, on basic skills for adults and on work-related skills. The infrastructure of adult learning, for many years a pillar of British education and widely admired throughout of the world, is being lost.

The book calls for urgent re-appraisal and better understanding of the public value of adult learning. Its contributors believe that creating and sustaining cultural value are as important as education for access to employment and workforce development. They campaign for continued educational opportunity for those who have been failed by our educational systems. The essays are wide-ranging, stimulating, and provocative. They make a convincing argument for a well-educated citizenry, empowered through learning to challenge bigotry, sophistry and injustice.

Foreword

David Sherlock (formerly Chief Inspector, Adult Learning Inspectorate)

Adult learning and the global economy

Chris Humphries (Director General, City and Guilds of London Institute)

The wider benefits of learning

Leon Feinstein (Director, Centre for Research on the Wider Benefits of Learning, Institute of Education, London University)

Adult literacy learning, participative democracy and public collective good
Ursula Howard (Director, National Research and Development Centre for Adult Literacy and Numeracy, Institute of Education, London University)

The right to make the wrong choices: liberty, choice and learning
Carole Stott and Finbar Lillis (Directors, Credit Works)

Demonstrating public value
John Stone (Chief Executive Officer, Learning and Skills Network)

Public value: international insights
Tom Schuller (Head, Centre for Educational Research and Innovation, OECD)

Adult learning and the local authorities
Richard Hooper (Manager, Adult and Continuing Education Services, Lancashire County Council)

Public value and leadership
Caroline Mager (Director for Strategic Policy, Centre for Excellence in Leadership)

Public value and Leitch
Duncan O'Leary (Researcher, DEMOS)

Learner perspectives
Richard Bolsin (General Secretary, Workers' Educational Association)

Adult learning and social justice
Nick Pearce (Director, Institute for Public Policy Research), Simon Beer and Jenny Williams (Regional Development Officers, NIACE)

Conclusion
Colin Flint and Chris Hughes